Dancing A Dizzy Holiness
Larry Janowski

First Edition
After Hours Press
Elmwood Park, Illinois
2019

Grateful Acknowledgments

A Writers' Congress: Chicago Poets on Barack Obama's Inauguration. DePaul University Poetry Institute, Chicago, 2008. "Election Night, Grant Park, Chicago, 2008"

After Hours: A Chicago Journal of Poetry and Art, Chicago. 2000-2019. "Am I Standing in Your Light?", "Contempt," "Crash," "Dancing Through the Mandala," "Danseur," "Face Down," "Securities," "Severe Thunderstorm Warning," "Traffic Stop," "Vanceberg, Kentucky 1980"

America: The National Catholic Review. Boston, 2000. "Resurrection"

Journal of the Franciscan Federation and the Association of Catholic Colleges and Universities, Lodi, New Jersey, 2012. "Confessional Poem" and "Communion Procession"

Poets Club of Chicago 78th Anniversary Anthology. Chicago. 2014. "Small Class Photo"

RHINO, Evanston, Illinois. "Religious Poem" 2012; "Thirteen Ways of Looking at a Short Guy," 2010

Vision. TrueQuest Communications, Chicago. Winner Best Original Poem, 2009, National Religious Vocation Conference. "Just Take It"

And most of all, thanks to a group of amazing, generous, patient, prize-winning Chicago poets and friends: Albert DeGenova, Pat Hertel, Nina Corwin, Patricia McMillan, Chris Green, Jan Bottiglieri, Bonnie Summers, Tony Trigilio, the Poets Club of Chicago and many others. You are great.

Dancing A Dizzy Holiness
Larry Janowski
ISBN 978-0-578-56655-9
Copyright © 2019 After Hours Press
www.afterhourspress.com

All rights reserved. No part of this book may be reproduced in any manner (except brief quotations for review purposes) without the written permission of the author.

*For my family in Saint Francis of Assisi,
who said of his first beloved ragtag companions,
"And God gave me some brothers."*

Table of Contents

Cover Photo by P. Hertel

Introduction
    by Judith Valente 8

A Man of The Cloth
    Religious Poem 13
    The Blessing Of "Baubo's Garden – Everything Intimate" 14
    Maundy 16
    Abuse 17
    The Bushes: Gage Park, Chicago, 1951 18
    Confessional Poem 20
    Communion Procession 21
    Dancing Through The Mandala 22
    Severe Thunderstorm Warning 24

Coming Up Short
    Thirteen Ways Of Looking At A Short Guy .28
    Small Class Photo 30

The City
    Traffic Stop 34
    Crash 35
    It's Spring In Chicago 36
    Connection Has Been Lost 37
    Chicago Caravan 38
    Election Night: Grant Park, Chicago, 2008 .40

The Waning Crescent
    Life Expectancy 44
    Three Poems For The Kind Of Sick 45
    For The Left Hand: Meditation While Stuck In The Carpal Tunnel . . .48
    A Good Talking To 50

Family
    The Best Little Boy In The World 52
    Securities 54
    Contempt 56

	Three Hours With Dad	58
	When Mom Turned 90	60
	Common As An Old Lady	62
	Jacket And Tie	63
	Dressing Dad	64
	A Fine Sadness	65
Love		
	I Love You Too	68
	Resurrection	70
	First Light	71
	Am I Standing In Your Light?	72
	Vanceberg, Kentucky 1980	74
	I Do Not Fall In Love Anymore	75
	Danseur	76
	Tomorrow and Tommorow and...	78
Grace		
	Skin: A Letter	80
	Rain Work	82
	Face Down	84
	Just Take It	85
	Name Dropping	86
	The Priest Poet At Matins	87
	Grace	88

About The Poet 90

Judith Valente

Introduction

The finest poems offer us a clarifying vision of what it means to be alive. Larry Janowski is a poet who offers us a window – freshly washed, sparkling in its clarity – in which to view and revel in our common humanity. He is at once the chronicler of the modest and the messy. A poet of the mean and the immeasurable, the unfathomable and the absolutely mundane, the sorrowful and the glorious.

Whether he is sitting at the bedside of a dying parent, contemplating the lives of two elderly women in mismatched clothing inching across a city street, or brooding over his height (roughly the same as the Marquis de Sade), we are more than willing to go along for the journey with this most companionable of guides.

In many ways, Janowski shares much with two of his poetic heroes, Gerard Manley Hopkins and Walt Whitman. All three are writers with the capacity to see the real beyond the real, the hidden wholeness in our scattered lives, the transcendent in the ordinary.

Like Hopkins, who was a Jesuit priest, Janowski too has a twin vocation as a Franciscan friar and poet. "I hear you secretly groaning/ JesusChrist– not religion," he writes in "Religious Poem." What interests him is the root meaning of religion – the ligament of it -- the stuff that binds bone to bone, body to soul, human to human. He assures us, his work is not sermons in poetic clothing. Without ligature, he reminds us, we fall too steeply into our lost and isolated selves. Much of contemporary poetry runs away as fast as it can from any suggestion of God, spirit or soul. Janowski's poems embrace our innate spiritual yearnings fearlessly.

Unlike Hopkins, who was tortured by the pull between poetry and his priestly life (Hopkins on his death bed begged his religious superiors to burn his poems), Janowski moves easily between his dual callings, the way an Olympic swimmer switches seamlessly from breaststroke to backstroke. Like Whitman, he is the voice of the everywoman and everyman. The father who prefers polo shirts for their fewer buttons, but nonetheless eschews t-shirts. A black child wounded by a rock thrown during an open housing march. A mother who at 90 worries about looking old.

Like the bard of Brooklyn, Janowski is also a poet of place. His muse is Chicago, where he was born and raised. It is a city that he shapes into poetry and the place that shaped him as a poet. His poem, "Communion Procession" is drawn from his time serving parishes in the bungalow and bratwurst neighborhoods of Chicago's northwest side. In it, he lovingly observes the motley flow of humanity streaming up the church aisle to receive communion from his hands. It is a love poem to the human condition. I often read "Communion Procession" at spiritual retreats I am asked to guide. It is usually the one thing people actually remember from the retreat.

Much of contemporary poetry lurks within the shadow side of human nature, or summersaults in clever word play, or else aims to reveal as little as possible of the poet's meaning. But poems don't need to be "fancy," as Mary Oliver famously said. Janowski's poems aren't fancy. Think of them as the kind of unpretentious work shirts you might see proud men wearing in Chicago's southside Polish neighborhoods, places so familiar to Janowski. That doesn't mean these poems are facile. Each carries its own beauty.

I finished this collection wanting for more. More time with this prophet of the quotidian. More time with the flawed and fascinating people who populate this collection. These are poems that will make you want to dance out of gratitude. That will fill your head with a dizzy holiness. And isn't that the best kind of holiness?

– Judith Valente
August, 2019

Judith Valente is an award-winning author, poet and Pulitzer Prize-nominated journalist. She is a sought-after speaker and retreat leader on such subjects as living a more contemplative life, discovering inner wisdom through poetry, and finding meaning in your work.

A Man of The Cloth

Religious Poem

I hear you secretly groaning, *Jesus Christ—
not religion!* Well, yes, but not a sermon
in poem's clothes, but the thick Latin root
of religion, the *lig* of it — as in ligament,
tough stuff that knits bone to bone, holds
organs in place. Friends sometimes say
I'm spiritual, not religious, and I get that:
soul as solo, no one else making my rules.
But I need a we, an us, to believe not just
in, but with. Like when you fall in love:
don't you want every soul on earth to dance
along and run hungry to your feast? I can't
make it without rites of words, of water
wash and welcome. Like Thomas, if I am
going to believe I need to jam my finger
into your wounds, feel the jolt and balm
of your touch on my sores. I need to sing
and keen, to pray in an incense cloud
of sweat, feel anointing oil smeared
on my head, to rip apart the loaf and
eat it with you getting drunk on wine-blood
together. Without that ligature I fall
so easily into myself, settle for my own
abstractions, which are always true,
so very true.

The Blessing Of "Baubo's Garden – Everything Intimate"

Bless all those who will use this shop, either as buyers or sellers, so that by respecting justice and charity, they will see themselves as working for the common good and find joy in contributing to the progress of the earthly city.
                                    The Roman Ritual – Book of Blessings

Fresh-paint smell of mauve walls barely dry. Boxes
scattered like unopened gifts. Priest, proprietor and
friends huddle to invoke a blessing, less upon racks

of *bustiers* than on the bodies who will wear them.
A little shop of seventy-times-seventy veils, exuberant
stuff intended to conceal – surely – and as surely

to be lifted. Baubo's Garden, named for a belly goddess
whose shape is as comic as her name: nipples for eyes,
vulva mouth, wriggling hips and swinging tits,

so cheeky she could shake even despairing Demeter
out of her grief for lost Persephone. "We've got your size
32AA to 44G, special orders available." So come in,

dance the aisles like Herod's Salome. The king
offered everything he could think of, even to half
his kingdom if only she would dance, but she

needed no persuasion to wrap herself in such scarves,
her lobes heavy with golden hoops, to swing her hips
and jangle brassy bracelets louder than finger bells.

What sprinkled holy water can further bless
what blesses us into being? We come from sperm
and egg, from love and lust, with no neat line

between. Nonetheless, let us pray: Hear us, O God!
as we remember that we are the lovely stuff beneath
your fingernails, back when you pronounced us

good, in your image female and male. Bless these colors
wild as Persian dervishes, *foundations, bridal
undergarments for the sophisticated, sensuous*

woman. Bless this tiny temple of teasing and joy,
of tulle and silk, gauzy chiffon, so sensuous we resort
to French: *camisole, negligee, peignoirs* the color

of the insides of peaches, chemises lavender as an eye's iris,
and all weightless as lashes. Bless what makes us blush
and laugh to think anything could be holier.

Maundy*

I confess I do not always love
being a priest, or maybe I still
don't know how to be one
like those revered reverends ever
in danger of believing their own
holiness, which is no way to talk
of centuries of precedence,
but there it is. A man of cloth

would better be a man of camel-hide,
dining on grasshopper-and-honey
sandwiches, whose one sermon
is *Repent*, endlessly repeated.
*Turn from hate. Heal what is
torn*, words aimed at no sinner
but himself. Naked in the Jordan,
he ought to be scrubbing
his own skin, all the while insisting
*I am not He, not He, not He, barely
good enough to untie His sandals.*

Isn't a priest called to wash the feet
of the weary and broken, to carry
burdens rather than levy them,
to anoint with our tears the ones
whom the high priests choose to shun,
to beg the sinner's mercy,
and dry his feet in our beards?

---

*Maundy Thursday is the Christian holy day falling on the Thursday before Easter commemorating the Last Supper of Jesus Christ; a ceremony of washing the feet of the poor.

Abuse

The priest was tall, dignified, refined. I
served Mass for him often, wondering
at the elegance of the satin vestments

draping in perfect folds. The way he sang
the chants, often rising to his toes
as if nudging heaven in ecstasy. I'd never

paid attention to anyone's hands before,
but the grace of his long fingers could
distract me from my Latin responses.

I was probably in the sixth grade, about
12 or 13, when I was walking home
from school, and Father drove by, stopped,

and asked if I wanted a ride home. *Sure,*
flattered that a priest knew me, and was
being kind. We chatted and he asked

the inevitable question, *What do you want
to be when you grow up?* but before –
with eager pride – I could reveal my dream –

to be a priest like you, Father – he added,
*because you sure won't make it on your
good looks.* And smiled.

The Bushes: Gage Park, Chicago, 1951

Dressed, but with a little pool-water in my ears,
I tell mom I'm going to explore the bushes,
and before she can say Be careful, I'm off
to follow dirt trails blazed by other kids' bikes
that snake through a small patch of woods.

He is a tower from nowhere, standing erect
and tall, high above me, like the platform
the lifeguards sit on, but old. I can tell
from his whispery voice.
                         His cowboy hat
interests me, but it's the silver belt-buckle
that holds my attention, a stallion rearing
on its hind legs, the flash of it exactly
level with my eyes. The man does not
bend down, doesn't touch me, just looms.

Through a gap between shrubs, I catch sight
of a woman with streaming blonde hair
on the opposite side of the bushes. I yell –
for no reason – *Hi, mom!*
                         Hushed and husky
a far away voice asks *Is that your mother?*

Now I am scared.
                Yeah, I lie, duck, and dash
toward the startled woman on her spread-out
blanket and plop down beside her. No one follows.

My real mother looks up from her magazine,
surprised to see me emerge from the thicket
holding the hand of a strange woman. *I got lost!*
getting good at lying. I say nothing of the man.

More than sixty years later, walking through
midnight, I lose my balance. Shadow edges
whip, scratch at me like thorns. My arms spring
to break the fall, but there is nothing to grasp, no
kind woman, no silver stallion to speed me away.

Confessional Poem

Ever wonder what it's like on the priest's side
of the screen in that small dark closet? Guys may
imagine it's like dirty secrets overheard in a bar.
It isn't. It's sliding open a small door to a swell
of sorrow – *heartily sorry*. The very first one
I heard was a kid, 12 or 13 I'm guessing. I was 26.
What did he confess? You forget immediately.

What you remember is not hushed lust, a lie,
but a wound-in-a-whisper, inches away, *This
is what I've done, or haven't. I am so sorry.*
Silence. I could barely speak, but felt the urge
to embrace him, to let him cry, to tell him
that in God's eyes, he is blindingly beautiful.
But what priest or pope has the right words?

What you do – seventy times seven times –
is listen, is judge not, is utter the shattering
I absolve. . . and hope your own lousy breath
can still lighten the unbearable weight of love.
You gulp the rush of cool air as one leaves
and another enters bearing the mirror of
your own fracture. It's something like that.

Communion Procession

He raises the eucharistic bread slightly and shows it to each one, saying: *The body of Christ.* The communicants reply: *Amen.*

The body of Christ . . .
   . . . must have been working in the garden
   . . . smells of playground sweat
   . . . is missing two fingers
   . . . must be six months pregnant
   . . . cannot look me in the eye
   . . . is still grieving his wife
   . . . has made three months of sobriety
   . . . has a baby in each arm
   . . . is growing her hair back
   . . . has a smile like fireworks
   . . . must be two inches taller than last week
   . . . has a son in Afghanistan
   . . . needs to come out of the closet
   . . . should have divorced him years ago
   . . . has hands nearly translucent
   . . . has been giggling all through Mass
   . . . tries hard to hide the Parkinson's
   . . . reminds me of my grandfather
   . . . has skin the color of coffee
   . . . still hasn't the knack of her wheelchair
   . . . has to let go of that anger
   . . . can't remember to turn off his cell phone
   . . . has more faith than I
   . . . surely mustn't realize what that T shirt says
   . . . is beautiful.
                                Amen.

Dancing Through The Mandala

Missouri toddler ruins monks' meticulous sand design with a little tap dance. (AP)

He pulls off shoes and socks, gets grit
between his toes sand-dancing, a two-foot
Astaire in soft-shoe shuffle, brushes
what eight Tibetan monks spent bent

days painting. Cordoned off in the middle
of Union Station, they have silently trickled
granules through tiny tubes and funnels
forming a fragile blessing built on sand —

of sand — meant to welcome the weary
traveler: *Pause and enter this geometry.*
Welcome to a house of wonder. Unsure
what's been roped off, when the mother

returns she ducks to retrieve her wayward
blue-and-yellow-footed child, regains her
young Son-of-Non-Attachment, and hustles
him out of video surveillance range.

The monks arrive to find a rainbow
smeared through their handiwork.
Neither angry, nor sad they start again.
We have only three days left. We shall

have to work harder. When complete,
they themselves will sweep it away,
donate grains for onlookers' gardens,
collect sand into silk-wrapped jars only

to pour it into the brown silt of the Missouri,
to flow on like compassion, to the Mississippi,
the Gulf, and all the oceans of all the planet.
Had the monks returned to find the boy

still spinning there, would they have
asked him to stop or hiked their saffron
robes between their legs and whirled
with him, dancing a dizzy holiness?

Severe Thunderstorm Warning

In effect for another half
century at the age of 67
I'm reaching a conclusion
Jesus was a sailor when he
walked upon the water
sings Cohen on the radio
only drowning men could
see him . . . my kind of prayer
though I admit it's dangerous
to drop Jesus into a poem
so I woke up sad today I
often do but this morning
I knew why I'm reading a lot
of novels lately and Behold!
revelation came unto me
that none of the characters
believes or if one does is
predictably quirky pathetic
downright nuts or we readers
are being set up to find out
he's a hypocrite the rain's started
but that's fiction real people
around me believe I think
that if there is a God it has moved
to the sky boxes if anywhere
and never was in the sweating
crowd in the cheap seats anyway
lightning now gales people
are running into this Starbucks

sloshing and laughing a bolt
nearby incredibly bright clear
pure a fire truck screams there's
sense in a soup kitchen clinic
or school but to stand here
everyday speaking ancient
words in front of a vanishing
choir maybe I should not say
the words I love and need
so much but hold them inside
to keep them from floating
away on exhaled and dying
breath it's been four decades
as a priest for Christ's sake
and here the skies are roiling
where is your faith, little man

Coming Up Short

Thirteen Ways Of Looking At A Short Guy

You say that I am—and I quote—like [sic] kind of short. But no, Young Sir! You are too simple. Why, why, you might have said...
      Act I Soliloquy. Cyrano de Bergerac, by Edmond Rostand

Arrogant
>I, Sir, were I as short as you,
>would commit suicide
>and jump from this curb!

Insolent
>You're so short you can swing your legs
>sitting on a phone book.

Curious
>How do you . . . you know . . .
>over the rim?

Kindly
>Oh well, you can rub shoulders
>with all of God's little creatures. Literally.

Diffident
>Sorry.
>I didn't see you.

Optimistic
>When it rains,
>you're the last to know.

Helpful
>Can I bring you
>a stool?

Pedantic

>Does not the alchemist Paracelsus
>claim a mythologic homunculus
>who stood no more than a foot tall?
>Surely here we have the original!

Eloquent

>Small
>but perfectly formed.

Enterprising

>Well, you can always buy your clothes
>in the boys' department.

Lyric

>Inside every grown man
>is ever a little boy.

Biblical

>For all have sinned and come short
>of the glory of God. (Romans 3:23)

Abashed

>Oh, I'm sorry.
>You are standing.

Small Class Photo

Okay, line up according to height. I'm sorry
you're always first, Alex Pope (4' 6"), but look
who your partner is: Ruthie Westheimer! She's got
an inch on you, but as she always says

"Size doesn't matter." Okay, Edith Piaf (4' 8")
you're with Robert Reich (4' 10_"), but Bobby,
don't let that two-and-a-half inches go
to your head — so to speak. Now, Francophones!

*Jeanne d'Arc avec Toulouse-Lautrec l'un
et l'autre* (4' 11"). *Bon!* Lovely couple. Hey!
DeVito, Daniel (5')! Hands off. She's a saint
for God's sake! And J.P. Sartre (5'), for pity's sake,

smile for the camera, okay? Johnny Keats (5' _")
you're next, then Fr. Hopkins with Bucky
Fuller, both (5' 2"), and then Prince formerly
known as Pee-Wee also (5' 2"). Don't ask me

what you have to talk about. How about
a dapple dawn-drawn falcon under a dome
geodesic? Yes, Truman Capote you will
make a trio between Saint Francis and that nice

Marquis de Sade, (all 5' 3"). Another 5' 4"
threesome: Moe Howard, if you lift
those bangs you'll see you've got
Louie-the-Bee on your left and Wolfgang

on your right. Wolfie, watch your mouth.
Now the "tall" guys Spike Lee and Tolkien (5'5")
in the back. No gloating, Furry Feet, or
I'll tell everybody what the J.R.R. stands for.

The City

Traffic Stop

Not so slowly as a tortoise or a wet weekend, but slow.
Two women, thin sisters in unmatched clothing, hair

the same fine-spun white gold, aware of the gravity
of choice, step into the crosswalk. Too old to believe

in safety between white lines, they unfold themselves
to full height, signal their grand progress—not so slow

as a boat to China or a mass of molasses, but slow indeed—
unperturbéd pace, deliberate speed, majestic instancy.

Ladies who once deemed speed unseemly now know it
to be impossible. Arms locked like twin ballerinas

or brides beginning down the aisle, free arms curved
above their heads like wispy arcs of scudding clouds

or white swan necks *en couronne*, they defy traffic
by grace alone, toss coquettish waves like blessings

from a two-headed faerie queen. We expect them
to pirouette and ourselves to applaud as they turn

and bow to us from at the far curb, then merge,
a single shadow beneath the elm trees.

Crash

Morning rush on LaSalle St. where any slow down
means thrombosis in arterial streets, not the place
for curbside service, but it happens so smoothly
not even cabbies have time to horn in. She pulls over
as he, tall and lanky, leaps out before the car stops
moving — intense, square-jawed — Clark Kent
in horn-rimmed glasses, jacket flapping in the cold,
but no hero. He bends, I am thinking, for a kiss, but
slams the door so hard my windows rattle. She,
young, blond, pretty, does not flinch
or look back, just trusts
her mirrors. She flows.
She goes.

It's Spring In Chicago

First day of spring: highs in the mid 40s. Snow after midnight 3 to 5 inches. Blustery.

It's the first day of spring
and I feel the urge to scour
corners, raise shades, vent
and illuminate. If windows
still had sashes and shutters
I'd throw them open. Come in!

It's the second day of spring
and snow needle-stings skin,
pillow-piles on sills. The dead sky
rattles. Laughs. The flow'ring
crocus croaks to budding daffodils:
Go back! Save yourselves! Go back!

Connection Has Been Lost

The average American adult checks his or her cell phone 50 times a day

Done with class at last, I'm as eager as my students
to feel this dazzling autumn sun and feel the breeze,
only to find I am not, after all, sharing anyone's

company. Most persons have vanished, clicked
their way into some otherwhere, a here
that isn't. My occasional smile bounces back,

as if from mirrored sunglasses, returns
like Noah's doves, having found no living thing
on earth. In poetry class, we mull over Forster's

Only Connect, but here, inches away from
one another; here, where Mountain Ash leaves
spin the air into gold, who notices glory?

Did our remarkable opposable thumbs evolve
thus far merely so we would not drop
our phones? Maybe further technological

advancement will mutate the gene into a
fully freakish 207th bone. This instrument
nestles the world in my warm palm unless

you reach for and take my hand and raise
my downcast eyes away from the small wall
of light in my private cave, lead me out.

Chicago Caravan

I pull in behind the hearse – privileged place for clergy or family – to form this vestige of village life, the funeral cortege, not on foot, casket hoisted upon our own bones and headed for the churchyard, but a long drive to where we keep our dead. We idle.

I remember

the days when my used-car-dealer dad would jam
three or four of us into his car for a drive
to who-knew-where to retrieve newly-purchased
stock. He never told us what he'd bought – so
during the drive out I'd imagine myself tooling
home in a little red TR3 convertible, only to be
entrusted with a tan Studebaker station wagon.

Across the city, our caravan of decrepitude –
the blind, the lame, the halt – faulty brakes,
spongy shocks, pistons missing, tailpipes
belching blue smoke – glued, nose-to-tail,
elephants or mules in the slow lane because
you never know with what is old.

                        We drive alert
for telltale engine ping, fan belt rattle, tappet
tic-tic-tic-tic ticking, smell of gasoline, anything
burning, or worst of all, a radio that doesn't play.
Dad – O my Captain – in the lead, and I
right behind, eyes on the dealer plates
spring-clipped to his bumper, first in his wake,

proud to anticipate his lane-changes,
my smooth moves running interference,
blocking so that he never has a blind spot
to worry about.

    Picture it! Four or five wheezy
vehicles turned into a formation of beauty —
the Blue Angels low and slow on the expressway!

A funeral procession weaving through Chicago
streets is a mournful accordion of gaps — first
wide as Mercutio's church-door wound — then
sudden squeezes for fear that our long line
of lamentation be severed leaving the tail
to hunt blindly for Resurrection Cemetery.

> *With dad in the lead on those last legs home,*
> *I never worried. Even if I got cut off by*
> *a traffic light or train, I knew that when*
> *cross-traffic cleared, or an endless freight*
> *had burst at last into silence and the red-swinging*
> *flasher was still, the gate would lift and he'd*
> *be there, idling at the curb not far ahead,*
> *engine throbbing, his large and beating heart.*

Election Night: Grant Park, Chicago, 2008

I wonder where she is tonight, the dark girl
I last saw lying still, bleeding on the front lawn
of a funeral home on South Kedzie Avenue,
a sunny Chicago afternoon, July or August,
1965. I was a kid-reporter, not even a cub,
for the Associated Press covering yet another
open-housing march, this one though in my own

neighborhood. The rock, undoubtedly hurled
by some neighbor's hand, was fully intended
to bash in heads, to draw blood. It did. She fell
as if deflated. I ran to her, but afraid to touch her
and make it worse, I ran into a drugstore and
called an ambulance, which seems funny now.
So many cops around. Didn't they see?

I did not sit beside her until help came. The march
was moving. I had to move with it. My job.
I remember her tonight, forty-three years later,
the bloodstained grass, how my own blood
has always stayed mostly inside my body, how
I've paid virtually nothing for the joy of this
warm November night, although I did keep
believing. That counts for something, I hope,

writing stories of witness, getting into it
with crimson-faced relatives, incensed that I
could side with them, people like her, this girl
I did not know. She is here tonight, somewhere
in Grant Park. I feel her in the wash of a different
kind of weeping. I'm here too, at the fringe
of this crowd, nothing in my hands but the sting
of applause, hopeful, still ashamed of that rock.

The Waning Crescent

Life Expectancy

A summer morning not far from Lake Michigan,
but the breeze cannot temper the heat rising
from black asphalt. It's another trip to Mercy.

Whatever the results of this latest –scopy, –gram,
or scan, the fact that I need it does generate an icy
counter to the heat and makes me shudder. Cancer. Again.

A strong stink as I step from the curb. The everyday
smells of Chicago have changed since I was a kid.
Instead of mud, hot weeds, creosote and sweet

bus fumes, it reeks now of sewage. The city can
no longer contain all our shit. Aging pipes
and tubes and tunnels are crumbling, too full,

too old to do their job. Last night a poet spoke
of death as a tolerable notion – that is – until
it shows up on your own block. My tiny

high school senior class of 26 is already down
by two: one, my best friend. I may have inherited
my nonagenarian parents' genes – dad's eyes,

mom's handwriting; his anger, her anxiety –
but I am not as strong. As they diminish, I am
being pared too, like the moon, shaved thinner
night-by-night, a waning crescent. A scythe.

Three Poems For The Kind Of Sick

1)

The seven signs of cancer we grew up
watching for included blood anywhere
it shouldn't be, which definitely includes
your pee. Sorry, but urine is too clinical
for the streaming shock. Stare. Silence,
the sudden stillness that follows
in the wake of I'm sorry to tell you;
silence, like a hum you're unaware of
until it stops. It is the sound your world
makes when it's halted for a moment
and before it resumes its turning, inexorable,
ready to go on without you at any time.

You grapple to hold on to something that
does not move, a chair, a hand, barely hearing,
caught early . . . treatable . . . surgery. You
contact friends, ask for prayers, and if they come
in a flood of kindness, promises to whisper
your name to God or the universe, even
from those who say they don't pray, but
their compassion will not allow them
to ignore your need. Now, embarrassed
by such concern, you want to say Never mind!

Save the prayers for somebody really sick,
someone bed-bound, because I am not.
Look! The bleeding has stopped. I'm fine.
Really. But too late because the great

up-draft of mercy set loose in the world
has jarred the cosmos, slowed its wheel
by dragging a foot the way we used to stop
a brakeless bike, jamming, skinning
the leather. "My mother will kill me,"
but it's downhill and I gotta stop!

Meanwhile God sort of wonders who
has been tilting His universe.

2)

Surgery. Recovery. Did they get it all?
Has it spread? You are embarrassed
to be feeling so well, start to believe

your own protests: Not so serious.
Really. Everything will go on as before . . .
except it isn't the same. You look at what

surrounds you in this room: the half-read
books, framed faces, stuff that should say
this space is yours, but it's all turned

useless, just the stuff you've been hauling
around even as you diminish and fade. You
smile at such drama. How operatic of me!

3)

You'll get a poem out of this, they say,
and they are right — at least in the
This-is-what-happened-to-me-and
here's-a-poem-I-wrote-about-it
School of Poetry, where you have long
been a member.
                      But what has happened
exactly? Have you sat down beside Death,
smiled and offered him root beer and a cupcake
even as your allotted four-score-and-ten
slip away rather more rapidly than you
would like?
                      The pathology is in at last,
and the doctor's "non-invasive" sounds like
the Huns have been turned away from Rome.
You are grateful the enemy is routed. You
are relieved in a sober kind of way. But your
Slavic melancholy insists that a reprieve
is the best you can do negotiating with God.

For The Left Hand:
Meditation While Stuck In The Carpal Tunnel

for Dr. Craig Phillips

They say I'll be typing again two weeks
after the snip of tendon. Release they call it,
the promise to unclog the words gridlocked
at the mouth of the tunnel like traffic jammed
on the Jersey side, words backed up for miles,
blowing their own horns trying to inch each other
out, growling, snarling, eager to surface
from under the dark river of the mind, break out
onto that wide other side, where

                              anesthesiacs dream
of nurses ... doctors ... everyone asks
which hand ... don't they know? ... an
X inked on the right ... I mean correct one ...
now I shall be sinister ... temporary
lefty ... like Mom until she taught herself ...
bounce and catch a ball in her right ...
like everyone else ... but if thy right hand ...
lead thee astray ... cut it off ...

                        In recovery,
"elevate the hand higher than your heart
to decrease the swelling ...", and I don't know
which I like better: the liquid sound
of *swelling*, or *Edema*—like a witchy mezzo
in a Verdi opera.

At home I can't wait
two whole weeks and begin to peck at the keys,
saying everything single-handedly. The lazy left
is clumsy as a soloist at first, but becomes
accustomed to the special attention. Fingers
warm up slowly under the heat of the spotlight,
begin to leap like Baryshnikov, show their stuff,
their unexpected and crackling grace.

A Good Talking To

Do not eat chocolate late at night, it's worse
than coffee for keeping you awake and alert
to the looming trail ahead marked "Oldmandom,"
over which a sign reads, *So? What have you done
with your one wild and precious life?*

Never having *whatthefuck*-ed, you've always been
too good for your own good. Your first grade nun
called you *Little Professor*. Why do you remember
that? You probably believed it, Buddy, but you're
not the best boy-in-the-world, and never were.

Get over it. Got a right to bitch because nothing
ever goes the way it should. Every right to be
angry? So does everyone else, Pal. Welcome to
the human race. You are not a special case.
So what? Want to slam doors, write nasty letters?

Go ahead, but for God's sake, Larry, make a little
happiness for yourself. And go back to sleep.

Family

The Best Little Boy In The World

The-best-little-boy-in-the-world wasn't good
enough for his father. That was bad, but
when the boy began to think maybe God
wasn't satisfied with him either, it hit hard,
because the boy had started to think about God,

and if he wasn't good enough for Him, then
the-best-little-boy was a fraud, flawed, scarred,
ugly, too blemished to make even a decent
lamb of sacrifice, not good enough even for
the knife. Of course, the boy never thought

about this until decades later when he was
neither little nor a boy, how back then, he
was a constant disappointment, unlike
the neighbor-kid, whose father had boasted
to the father of the-best-boy-in-the-world

that he, the neighbor, had the perfect son,
who not only *does whatever he's told.* He
doesn't even need to be told! Mr. Markevich
smiles and wraps his arm around his perfect son,
right there, in front of the father and his

failed best-boy, who could not remember
his father's arm on his shoulder. Ever. And
when the teenage best boy made a friend
he wanted to hang around with when he
should have been mowing the lawn: *You're . . .*

*selfish and lazy. And your friend is not that
important*, which kindled the kid's anger,
but that too was wrong so, still smoldering,
he swallowed hard, which made his father smirk,
so that the boy's eyes began to brim with memory

of the first time his father had shot his contempt
all through the house: *And stop carrying your
books like a girl!* At least no one had heard that,
except his mother. But still.

Securities

1)

grey-green
steel strong

box to hold
your paper

life, policies
adopted, deeds

done, profits
shared, stock

taken, trust
established,

debts paid
in full

months ago, your two sons spread out on
your living room floor to pore over paper
and sort into neat piles your 90 years — not just
what you'd secured in this chest on the closet shelf,
but stacks of tax returns, canceled checks, post-op
instructions for surgery you had thirteen
years ago, manuals for yet another
electric shaver and the electric toothbrush
you no longer need — your sons chose from what
you dropped at their feet like a retriever, we
decided what to save, what to shred.

2)

When we finished, we presented you with a new
file, streamlined, to keep you organized and
ordered so that we — whenever it would happen —
could easily find what we might need. Weeks later,
dad lifts the old box down from the closet shelf
in search of some creased memory only to find
none. Nothing. No bottom. Space so deep his
echo could not find its way out. Frantic with
your panicky call, your first-born speeds wildly
across the city, walks into your kitchen, welcome
as a shoplifter, helpless to make restitution

no explanation
no patient reminder

of that new
chest of neatly-

labeled color-
coded logic

can convince
you that

you are
still who

you have
always been

Contempt

This morning a country drive, explosions
of Redbud, Apple Blossom and Dogwood,
oohs and ahs from mom and dad under a mild,
true-blue sky. How — in the time it took
to drive them back to the retirement village,

go home myself and grade a batch of papers —
had spring turned to winter. The phone. "What
are we doing here?" Mom asks her months-
repeated fear: "Who's going to pay for all this?"
Assurance calms her, but minutes later

the phone again. Dad explodes: "How can you
do this to us? I've never been treated so bad
in all my life." *Must be a wrong number. Who
is this? Who am I?* I do not argue. "And you —
a priest! — You should be ashamed. Someday

you'll be sorry." *Someday?* My whole body shakes.
Forgotten are his falls, overdosed medications,
the confusion over whose neighborhood
he'd driven into. And he is not finished. "You
treat me like I'm losing my mind, and I'm not!"

We're all losing something. "Fine," he says,
"we'll just die here." I do not speak. *You
may be right.* "Goodbye, my friend,"
that last word an icicle. An hour later,
another call, his face on the small screen

on my phone. I shield myself. *Let it ring,*
but pick up, steeled. And then crumble.
Which is harder to hear? The eruption of
a father's contempt, or words he'd never
spoken to me before: "Can you forgive me?"

Three Hours With Dad

I thought he was dead when I walked in,
mouth open, eyes closed, no dentures.
Eventually he came around, groggy,

since he'd pulled out his IV overnight and
had to be sedated. Mom had returned
to their apartment. It was just he and I.

He talked. I sat close, held his hand.
His words were clear fragments, but not
threaded by logic, until "I don't know

what's happening to me. Am I losing
my marbles? I love you." And then
"I don't get it. Don't leave me. We have to

always stay together. Where is my wife?"
"Mom was here all day, Dad. She'll be back
tomorrow."
                "I have to get out of this bed."

With an edge, "No, Dad. You have to
stay here," embarrassed that I sounded
as though I were disciplining a feisty child.

Supper was beef stew. His shaking fingers
could not wrap around the spoon he was
using like a knife, so he used his hands,

gravy fingerprinting, as he tried to pick up
sauce with his fingers. I took the spoon
and fed him as I'd fed my baby brother

55 years ago. Unresisting, unembarrassed,
his mouth gaped for the next morsel until
"Enough." All through that first day I didn't
feel. No pity. No sadness, just What am I
supposed to do now?

When Mom Turned 90

"I look like an old woman," she said,
    unhappy with her last beauty shop
        visit. "You *are* an old woman,"
            Dad said, not without mischief, not
                without tenderness. We began to

keep an eye on her cholesterol,
    blood pressure and heart as she grew
        even shorter than her full five feet.
            Some things did not change, like
                the way she could remember lyrics

of songs from before the War, like
    "When they've all had their quarrels
        and parted / We'll be the same as we
            started / Just travelin' along, singin'
                our song / Side by side," and I'd sing

along. She re-told the same stories,
    like how – watching golf on Sunday –
        the ball came to rest at the lip of the cup,
            "and everyone was chanting 'Go in!
                Go in!' and it did!" Or how – during

a harrowing drive through Appalachia –
    dad dealt with dense fog by falling in
        behind the red tail lights of a semi
            to guide them down the mountain,
                a vein in his forehead pulsing as her

heart throbbed along, and she loved him
    all the more. A simple woman, who
        atop Lookout Mountain in Tennessee,
            saw the world from a new height and
                whispered "There must be a God."

One Mother's Day my sentimental
    card gushed over her innumerable virtues,
        and she said – perfectly seriously – "Well,
            some of it's true and some of it isn't."

Common As An Old Lady

like a she-bear
spring-roused, not sure
where she is or why she is
awake. Thin,
        sucked dry,
so she no longer rumbles the ground
but pads the den floor to nuzzle her cub.
She is at less than half her weight, at
half her hemoglobin
half her potassium
the doc says *We have a problem.*

I sit with her, grow tired and bored
holding her hand, and remember
an oft'-sung sad and scary lullaby
Put My Little Shoes Away that she used to
sing, knowing I would cry, and she would
comfort me. Training.

Lately, every morning, they find her crumpled,
sitting or kneeling on the floor beside her bed,
not sure where she is or why she is, not praying,
but looking for her shoes.

Jacket And Tie

I wore a jacket and tie today, first day
of school, not to make an impression –
college students are not easily impressed –

but for me. I like a man in a tie, professional.
Sometimes I even put on a tie working
at home! What my father used to call

looking sharp. *I'll drop in on mom
on the way home*, I think. She likes
to see me dressed up. She'll notice

the new tie, teal, with a whispery rose
pattern, dove gray shirt. At 95, she
will say, "You look so good!"

To make her happy makes me happy.
She has little joy these days, a widow
for a just a few weeks, hardly long enough

to feel dad's absence beside her.
Suddenly my plan – crammed into
an instant's thought – shatters.

Oh. She's gone too. I do not feel like crying,
just transparent, as if no one will ever
truly see me again, necktie or not.

Dressing Dad

I began doing my parents' laundry, my bit to assist
their living, though there was not much to wash,
content as they were with the well-worn and comfy.

It was strange for a celibate to deal with panties,
for any son to discover that — like a hippie, decades
too late for the 60s Revolution — mom had gone braless.

Sometimes dad's shorts were stained. He liked polo shirts,
fewer buttons to fumble with, yet a little dressier
than a T-shirt. I bought him several, a variety of colors,

but he looked best in blue and wore that one all the time.
One of Mom's oft-repeated memories: I must have read it
somewhere, but they asked people 'What's your favorite

color?' and everybody said blue! I bought an identical
shirt for myself, but in the confusion of laundering,
lost track of whose was whose. He and I were now wearing

the same size, like roommates or brothers. I buried
my father in my own black suit. It fit him, more or less,
a man who — all my life — had been inches taller than I.

He was dressed in his own white shirt and shoes,
but my tie. Belt. Socks. Underwear.

A Fine Sadness

How are you?
  Finehowareyou?
    Fine.

F-ucked up / I-solated / N-eurotic / E-gotistical,
but *fine* will have to do because I refuse to say

I'm sad today.

Sad makes people squirm, eager to change the subject
or the bar stool, since fun is the one criterion by which
things are judged. But isn't life "this vale of tears,"
as in the old prayer? Maybe that's where Catholic Kerouac
found his sweet sadness, sad occurring 82 times in *On the Road*.

If it weren't for sadness, what feeling would I have?
Anger frightens me and "Happiness" often merits
its scare-quotes, real as "The Big Rock Candy Mountain."
At least sad is honest. Yes, loss is constant. But it is
not a pit, but only a pool, too shallow to wallow in,

but deep enough to soak you through. So why am I
writing this poem? Slavic Angst? Or am I just being
lugubrious? (What a word!) Of course, I do often
wake up muttering *I'm sorry. I'm sorry. I'm sorry.*
apologizing to God or to myself.

Love

I Love You Too
while watching 60 Minutes, *December 2, 2018*

                    The dying president's last words were to his son. "I love you."
"I love you too."

automatic echo, presumed, expected,
husks of words, inconsequential as

        "Hihow'reyou?"
        "Finehow'reyou?"

weightless breath, hardly heard
background chatter.

I love you . . .

Everything depends
(funny word, depend: to hang down
like fruit from a low branch)
everything hangs on
for dear life, waits

to either fall to the worms
or
be plucked, savored,
and bitten to yield sweetness
and juice.

But let's say that "I love you too,"
fully intends to mow you down,
to lay you low,
to leave you breathless

as it comes
screeching
around the corner on two wheels,
to grab you by the shoulders,
to shake you,
to look you in the eye
to make sure you hear
and understand

that words have
pierced your armor,
have penetrated your defenses
with the utter conviction
of a father's last words.

Who would have thought
that there is such
careful, sacred work
to listening

for the universe's
quantum shift

on *60 Minutes*,
on CBS,
on a Sunday night?

Resurrection

Thin as skin behind a knee,
transparent as the shadow
of a dragonfly wing — on such paper
Michelangelo sketched Tityus
prone and languishing

between visits from the vulture.
One day, full of un-Zeus-like
compassion, the master carries
the broken Titan to the window
and presses black chalk lines

up against rippled glass so daylight
can wash through the drawing
which he's rotated now, so that
the figure stands upright. Then,
on the verso (he does reposition

the legs), he traces the figure otherwise
unchanged: broadly muscled, naked,
unbound, bursting — now become
the Resurrected Christ. And
the world ignites like tinder.

First Light

O Love, your kiss rouses me
like a sleepy-headed youth
yawning awake to behold
the dark sky break into pieces.

O Love, stretch your body
toward clouds, thin, blue
and layered like smoke,
a shock against the black sky

where you pace the ridge
of dawn drawing to yourself
the first light until you are
flame. Your hair – O Love –

and eyes dazzle me. Who
can bear to look at you?
Come to me. Burn away
sleep until I am – like

Alexander's Hephaestion –
utterly consumed by you.

Am I Standing In Your Light?
for Tom

Somewhere I got a whiff today
of old fashioned Coppertone –
the kind with no SPF whatever –
the kind that could oil-slick
the air as much as the surface
of the pool at the El Sombrero
Motel in Miami Beach in 1955
where I posed pale for a picture
with tanned and handsome
Clyde Beatty, the famous lion tamer

(who was the first to use a chair
in the ring and was at the motel
with his secretary). In the sunken
lobby were three enormous
portholes. From there, I could watch
the thighs of swimmers from below.
Sometimes, at night, in the corners
of the pool, where turquoise and rose
spotlights didn't shine, they would
kiss underwater. You could see.

Not all people take good pictures,
not even famous ones. It's not about
pretty. Photography favors
the exaggerated: pronounced jaws,
outlandish cheekbones and lips,
and shadows, so that if you meet
someone famous in person, you're

surprised how faded he seems. There's
this old Polaroid I have of Tom. We
are 19, in the alley behind my garage.

The sun is going down, and the last
gash of gold catches him slouching
and splendid against the primered
'56 Olds we built together, his right
arm draping the car like a best friend's
shoulder. His sweat-shiny chest is
flecked with grease and he has a rag
bunched in the hand at his waist.
There is a shadow at his feet. He
is alone. I am taking the picture.

Vanceberg, Kentucky 1980
for Ted

Two creeks wash the mountain down,
rush to us who slip on slick stones
toward filtered forestlight. Spring
in Eastern Kentucky hollers, warm,
but not enough yet for snakes,
you say. The spaniel is already panting

in the clearing. We light a fire, pitch
the tent. You brought your guitar, so
we sing old hymns, invent odd new
harmonies—something like the friendship
we've cobbled together this past year.
Our voices drown in the sound gushing

from two gashes in the earth, but you
go on singing a song you wrote for
someone I don't know. We eat. Drink.
Laugh. Pray for good futures we will
navigate alone, because we're headed
in opposite directions. The day ebbs,

and firelight casts our shadows against
the tent. They flicker, merge, move apart
in this greenly cool, where two creeks
meet. We trail our hands into the dark,
flowing water, but it is blue cold. We
pull back.

I Do Not Fall In Love Anymore

and haven't for a long while.
I do miss how such falling feels —
like the joy of a puppy, all saliva
and pee, and no notion of reality
or consequences — but it's never
turned out well, has it?

When out of the cold night you
stunned me saying *Larry, you know
that I love you*, I lost my equilibrium,
hardly believing those words came
first from you. But that summer,
came the *I'm sorry, Larry, but I* . . .

I do still love — more often,
more deeply than ever — but
I am more circumspect, pausing
carefully in both the uttering and
the reply. After all, I am old,
and falling is very dangerous.

Danseur

Squat. Nothing lithe or graceful
about my body. Even if I'd had
the notion to enroll, no teacher
would take me as a student.

Polka-plodding was all I'd managed
growing up: spinning, stomping,
whooping. Amazement at what
a body and music could create
came much later, not just a desire

for ballroom dance, but more
outrageous, ballet! where dancers
Grand Jeté into a lover's arms. Where
a ballerina spins on a single toe

so fast her revolutions can't be
counted. She does not dizzy,
though once, backstage, I saw
Nureyev dash into the wings,
vomit, and with perfect timing,
leap back to the stage to lift
the feather body of his *Giselle*,
then fade into the scenery
so that our attention was only
upon her weeping body until she
soared again, and finally settled
with the delicacy of a dragonfly
on the tip of a fishing rod.

And the men. Their beauty:
sheer, shining, sweating muscle,
bellies that have never known
a pillow of fat. To be such a body!
To touch one, to be touched,
lifted, balanced at my fulcrum
and cancel my burden of bulk;
to run, be caught, draped from
another *danseur's* arms, then
weightlessly fall into them.

Tomorrow and Tomorrow and...

Just to start is the hard part, Jesus said — or
was it Jimmie Dodd on the Mickey Mouse Club?

Whoever it was, deep in my 12-year-old soul,
I knew it was true, the way the Golden Rule

was true, but hard. I knew the truth, but it didn't
set me free, but only ground guilt into the wound

of not-beginning-until-there-is-nowhere-else-to-go.
Pencils down! Time's up! You're too late!

Maybe that is why I cannot bring myself
to deduct points for late essays, despite my

No extensions! Like today — windows
washed, laundry folded, shoes shined,

floors waxed, papers graded, groceries
bought, bills paid, thank you cards mailed —

having run out of things I must do first, I still
can't make myself drive those few miles,

drag the folding chair from the trunk to where
you lie, set it on the uneven ground — already

covered in wet, slippery, yellow leaves under
a dust of snow — and tell you how much I . . .

But tomorrow I will. I promise.

Grace

Skin: A Letter

> *His high school nickname was "Skin," and even now at age thirty-one [Gerard Manley Hopkins] weighed hardly a hundred pounds, with a jockey's height of five feet four. (Ron Hansen.* Exiles*)*

Every photograph of you – sad, even when you're smiling – beyond the sobriety
of sitting for a photograph – betraying a struggle, perhaps a shock, to find the Society
of Jesus so strenuous even beyond the vows. I understand. We have in common

more than being born exactly a century apart: poets, priests, teachers, gay men
– four vocations (is it a gift to be gay?) though I order them differently
than you, compelled as you are always to place priest ahead of poet; Jesuit and priest

above all things for God's sake, ferocity of faith, military discipline, manly,
Manley, your God in khaki, your soutane ablaze with medals for bravery
under flesh-fire. Dear friend, may I call you that? today I invite myself

into your century, your company, not for long, but long enough to greet you, to kiss
your hands and to introduce a friend whom I shall bring along. You know him,
at least of him. And he will be happy to meet you, though you call him *scoundrel!*

a word you used, I must believe, with a wry smile. His name is Whitman.
Since I come from the future, and you are both in my past, we will doubtless
find one another curious. You in black, I, in brown, and Walt chuckling

at us in his disheveled workingman's clothes, hat jauntily tilted. Yet whether
nineteenth century Britain or 21st century America, you and I and the old man
will still be queer, for so we are, the three of us, the oddness that cuts deep

and makes us see beauty and desire and open hands. And so, dear Gerard,
we shall embrace, you and I – no longer touch-starved – if only for a time
– and we will praise God for skin in our maddening celibate way. "Hey, Hopkins!

Hey, Skin!" And we will swim together, but you will have to teach me, for I am
frightened of water as you are of sin, and – dare I say – sometimes of your self.
Walt will watch us, the beautiful boys we were, at swim, relishing our nakedness

when we set aside these habits of self-doubt, of fear and shame. Old Walt will
guard our clothes and chastity, but not at the cost of our touching, holding
our pale selves, face to face in water, Gerard, and we will allow our eyes

out of custody, aware and thrilled we're both of us men. Perhaps you and I
will take Walt's hands, disrobe him. At nearly 70, his is still the body electric.
Piece by piece we will doff his shirt and trousers, pull him into the water

with us, laugh and splash at the good we are. But when we emerge, it will be
you and I who shall dry one another's hair, and lie down together, content.
Or maybe we will weep for the beauty-brevity of it all, the whole length

of our small bodies grieving. But for that moment, it will be you and I,
sweet friend, my poet, my brother, loosely holding hands, leaving God to judge
and Walt to write the poem.

Rain Work

*You cannot save yourself, but nothing is
impossible for God* — who arrives arm-in-arm
with Shakespeare and a passel of other poets
all of whom appear to be chatting about me
in an oddly companionable way.

Their arrival comes on the heels of a nightmare
in which the sins of my life paraded before me,
and in obedience to some sergeant angel's
"Eyes right!" obediently turn to stare blankly at me.

I ran outside into the warm, wet night, praying
that the bitter taste in my soul be scoured
along with all the sins of commission, omission
and narcissism I've talleyed. Do they come
with divine judgment? In answer, Isaiah
the poet-prophet says he has been eaves-
dropping on God and announces in his stentorian voice
what he has overheard Him say.

> *My every Word is like the rain or snow
> that would not dare return to me empty,
> but only once it has accomplished
> the work for which I sent it — in your
> case to bear mercy to the earth, there to
> be twice blessed. My word is mercy,
> and it falls like this gentle rain blessing
> and being blessed for what it has brought*

*to us: seed for the sower, bread for the
one who eats, and mercy for the one who
has strayed.*

And suddenly I am sluiced, as if in used
baptismal water, dark and heavy with the grit
of a lifetime.

Unbelieving but hoping, I pray that my miserable old
sins have got the message that Grace truly is amazing.
Mud oozes between my
toes as I recall the final words of one
of Hopkins' sonnets, that aching, desperate
plea, "Lord of life, send my roots
rain."

Face Down

When the last black-burnished mound of roadside snow
surrendered, it yielded – like receding tide – the corpse
of a stuffed toy that lay face down for several days more,
Winnie the Pooh, I think, to judge from yellow bear

body and faded red jacket, though no next of kin
came to claim the body. Was there a child missing
him, scouring neighborhood alleys, dragging
the kiddie pool? Or had there been an argument?

Had Pooh displeased? Deserved getting tossed out
of a passing car or pram, discarded in disgust, or rage?
Maybe he jumped. Why do we let go of what we'd held
so tight and so long that no breath could pass between us?

Maybe we don't let go, but are abandoned. Maybe it's easier
to lie in mud face down than to be so desperately loved.

Just Take It
on Robert Frost's "The Road Not Taken"

They love it. My students memorize the words,
but miss the point about that less-traveled road,
claim Frost a hero for endorsing the holy My-way,
though he called this poem a tricky one, very

tricky – less about not following the crowd or
which path to take – more about just making up
your mind. If he could, the poet would nod
to Yogi Berra: If you come to a fork in the road,

take it. In the end, there will always be those
two paths: the one you chose and the other one.
Pick one, I tell them, one that loves you back,
and if you still seek Yankee wisdom, read

the one about not standing and staring
too long, about miles to go and promises.

Name Dropping

That's a cheap applause line! You can throw 'Jesus' into anything, and people are going to applaud.
    – Stephen Colbert to Sister Helen Prejean

"Jesus" stuck into a poem is like an alabaster jar
crashing to the floor at dinner . . . first silence,
then squirming. *Jesus* stops me too, though I
can toss his name about glibly, profanely
as a mechanic's five-letter word. Yet even

millennia later, his name still ignites, realigns.
At the University of Iowa, I sat in on a class
to hear a wildly popular Jewish professor, his
class jammed even with students not taking
his course. He was explaining Tetragrammaton,

the four Hebrew letters that make up God's name,
a name never to be spoken aloud. Whenever he
came to that word in a lecture, he would babble
nonsense syllables instead. And the class — far
from laughing — would fall still and silent.

The Priest Poet At Matins

I've shaped my life around a passion
called God. So if, in the night, I were

shaken awake as if by a persistent friend —
Get up, we need to talk — of course

I'd get up, groggy, but willing enough
to make coffee, sit down at the kitchen table,

and listen. Praying, after all, is mostly listening,
and poetry is paying attention. So I get up,

grope for my glasses — why do I need glasses
to listen? — piously ready to attend to

someone knocking at my soul's back door.
But also wide awake is my evil twin making

finger-horns behind my head while I try
to come up with clunky metaphors for this moment —

a kiss? A koan? Mud wrestling? But truly,
my deepest longing right now (O Lord, have mercy

on my soul!) is for God to hold on a minute
and help me find my damned pen.

Grace

           is enough time
to finish what you've begun,
even when debts are due
and you've already had more
than your fair share of laughter
and open-mouthed kisses,
evenings turned to night
at the shore shivering together
under blanket-hoods, sips
of cold water that hurt your teeth,
yet another birthday iris
in February. One more.
One more.

Grace
        is an egret,
its pace
and halt balanced
on toes that curve
upward like bowls
of water on the shore;
        is two legs of skin

painted onto bone and sinew,
knee joint like the node
of a chalice that holds
the whole cup
of feather-draped breast;

        it is the neck's S
tapering to a holy eye:
        the economy
of step
and stare.

About The Poet

It was under the Italian sun at Grecchio that Franciscan poets Murray Bodo and Larry Janowski had a frank discussion about the writing life, Janowski recalls. "In the early 1980s, I was a young priest and Murray was already a superstar among Franciscan men and women, having published a life of Saint Francis (*Francis: the Journey and the Dream*) as seen through the eyes and told in the language of a poet—which has sold over 200,000 copies.

"Back then I wouldn't have dared to call myself a writer, let alone a poet. So you can imagine that I was both shy and eager to ask the great man what every fledgling writer wants to know: 'Am I any good?'" Murray enthusiastically recommended I earn an MFA in creative writing, and I'd find out. And that's what I did."

Janowski chose to write fiction, and his mentors at Vermont College of Fine Arts would often require him to read novels and short stories that delved into the darker side of the human psyche. "I think they believed that a priest's writing would tend to be naive about the grittiness of real life."

Larry enjoyed some success in short fiction in magazines such as *Praying* (St. Louis) and *The Critic* (Chicago), *Literal Latte* (New York). Awards included a residency at the Blue Mountain Arts Center, Blue Mountain Lake, N.Y., an Artist Development Grant from the State of Wisconsin, and similar grants from the Illinois Arts Council and the City of Chicago Department of Cultural Affairs.

But before long, his writing energy began to move toward poetry. At a workshop in Kalamazoo, Michigan, Janowski met fellow Chicagoan, the amazing poet Edward Hirsch (*How to Read a Poem and Fall in Love With Poetry*). Larry recalls that when he told him about switching from fiction to poetry, Hirsch replied "Of course, you moved to a higher moral plane!" Larry says he is not sure about that higher moral plane, "but I am certain that language and poetry have drawn me closer to other human beings and thus to God."

According to Janowski, Saint Francis loved poetry that he heard from the 12th century troubadours and the French songs he'd learned from his mother. "Saint Francis' own greatest poem was not the famous 'Peace Prayer,'"says Larry, " but 'The Canticle of the Sun' in which he praises God for all of creation and encourages all creatures to be what they are. So much of my poetry is not typically 'religious' at all, but I try to see the goodness, the holiness in simply being alive. Rabbi Abraham Heschel says 'Just to be is a blessing, just to be is holy.'"

"At 75," Janowski says, "I could be winding things up as a writer, rather than publishing a new book, but before I unplug my laptop, I still have a lot to learn, or as the Acts of the Apostles puts it: 'In the last days it will be, God declares, that I will pour out my Spirit upon all flesh . . . your young men shall see visions, and your old men shall dream dreams."

Janowski has published two chapbooks, *Celibate Dazzled* and *Chicago Cantata*, and a full-length book, *BrotherKeeper* (The Puddin'head Press, 2007). He was born in Chicago where he taught at Wilbur Wright Community College, Dominican University, and Loyola University. He now lives near La Crosse, Wisconsin. Larry is a Franciscan friar.

www.ingramcontent.com/pod-product-compliance
Lightning Source LLC
Chambersburg PA
CBHW062028290426
44108CB00025B/2820